Author:

Ian Graham studied applied physics at the City University, London. He then took a postgraduate degree in journalism, specializing in science and technology. Since becoming a freelance author and journalist, he has written more than one hundred children's nonfiction books.

Artist:

David Antram was born in Brighton, England, in 1958. He studied at Eastbourne College of Art and then worked in advertising for fifteen years before becoming a full-time artist. He has illustrated many children's nonfiction books.

Series creator:

David Salariya was born in Dundee, Scotland. He has illustrated a wide range of books and has created and designed many new series for publishers in the UK and overseas. He established The Salariya Book Company in 1989. He lives in Brighton, England, with his wife, illustrator Shirley Willis, and their son Jonathan.

Editor: **Stephen Haynes**

Editorial Assistants:
Mark Williams, Tanya Kant

© The Salariya Book Company Ltd MMVIII
No part of this publication may be reproduced in whole or in part, or stored in a retrieval system, or transmitted in any form or by any means, electronic, mechanical, photocopying, recording, or otherwise, without written permission of the publisher. For information regarding permission, write to the copyright holder.

Published in Great Britain in 2008 by
The Salariya Book Company Ltd
25 Marlborough Place, Brighton BN1 1UB

ISBN-13: 978-0-531-20823-6 (lib. bdg.)   978-0-531-21049-9 (pbk.)
ISBN-10: 0-531-20823-0 (lib. bdg.)   0-531-21049-9 (pbk.)

All rights reserved.
Published in 2009 in the United States
by Franklin Watts
An imprint of Scholastic Inc.
Published simultaneously in Canada.

A CIP catalog record for this book is available
from the Library of Congress.

Printed and bound in China.
Printed on paper from sustainable sources.

SCHOLASTIC, FRANKLIN WATTS, and associated logos are trademarks and/or registered trademarks of Scholastic Inc.

Drone Drone

Squawk!

Oink!

You Wouldn't Want to Be on the Hindenburg!

Written by
Ian Graham

Illustrated by
David Antram

Created and designed by
David Salariya

A Transatlantic Trip You'd Rather Skip

Franklin Watts®
An Imprint of Scholastic Inc.
NEW YORK • TORONTO • LONDON • AUCKLAND • SYDNEY
MEXICO CITY • NEW DELHI • HONG KONG
DANBURY, CONNECTICUT

Contents

Introduction

The year is 1936—and this is the most exciting day of your life! You have just learned that you are to join the crew of the *Hindenburg* airship. The LZ129 *Hindenburg* is the world's biggest airship. It's as big as an ocean liner, but it's lighter than air, thanks to the hydrogen gas that fills it. It was built by the Zeppelin company in Germany for luxury flights across the Atlantic Ocean.

You have been working as an airship mechanic for the past five years. Your job is to keep the engines in tip-top condition. At first, you worked in workshops on the ground. Then you flew in the company's smaller airships, looking after the engines during flights. Now, you've been given your dream job in the brand-new *Hindenburg*. It is due to make ten flights from Germany to the United States and seven to Brazil, all in its first year. You'll be going with it— and you can't wait!

> I've always dreamed of being a high-flyer.

WHY *HINDENBURG*? The airship is named after Paul von Hindenburg, president of Germany from 1925 to 1934.

WHY HYDROGEN? Many airships are filled with helium gas. But the United States controls the supply of helium and doesn't want to sell any to Germany, so the *Hindenburg* uses hydrogen instead. Hydrogen works just as well as helium, but it has one major disadvantage: it burns easily.

5

Flying Whales

This armed French airship was used by the British in World War I to protect the English Channel.

Zeppelin airships have been flying since 1900. They are named after Count Ferdinand von Zeppelin, the German nobleman who developed them. Earlier airships were just big bags of gas; they sometimes collapsed like leaking party balloons. Count Zeppelin's airships are bigger and stronger because they have a metal frame inside. In 1909, Zeppelin formed Delag, the world's first airline. Its airships have carried tens of thousands of passengers—including you—between German cities. The Zeppelin company makes military airships, too.

THE FIRST AIRSHIP was built in France by Henri Giffard. It was 144 feet (44 m) long and powered by a steam engine. On September 24, 1852, Giffard climbed aboard and made the world's first airship flight.

Look out below!

DURING WORLD WAR I (1914–1918), the Germans used airships to drop bombs by hand onto enemy cities.

THERE WERE FEW anti-aircraft guns during World War I, but artillerymen could fire at airships by tilting the barrels of their field guns up high.

Handy Hint

If you want to work in an airship, make sure you're not afraid of heights!

ZEPPELINS were as big as ocean liners. If they were still flying today, they would dwarf modern airliners like the Boeing 747.

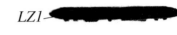

LZ1

LZ129 Hindenburg

Boeing 747 (Jumbo Jet)

RMS Titanic

THE AIRSHIP *AMERICA* tried to fly across the Atlantic Ocean in 1910, but it failed because its engines broke down. The crew and their cat were rescued by a passing British ship, the SS *Trent*.

FERDINAND VON ZEPPELIN spent a fortune building his first airship, the LZ1. No one believed this retired army officer could do it. People were amazed when he succeeded.

Ferdinand von Zeppelin

Building a Giant

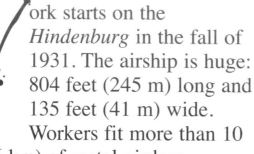

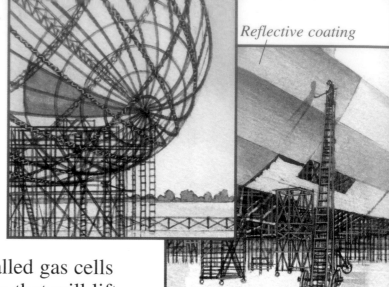

Reflective coating

 ork starts on the *Hindenburg* in the fall of 1931. The airship is huge: 804 feet (245 m) long and 135 feet (41 m) wide. Workers fit more than 10 miles (16 km) of metal girders together to form the airship's frame. Then 16 enormous drum-shaped bags called gas cells are installed. They hold the hydrogen gas that will lift the giant airship. Finally, the frame is covered with fabric and painted. It is finished by the spring of 1936.

Gas cells are held in place by a web of netting and bracing wires.

Rudder *steers the airship to port (left) or starboard (right).*

Elevator *helps to move the airship up or down or keep it level.*

Landing wheel *supports the airship when it is on the ground.*

Engine car: *four engines power the Hindenburg's propellers.*

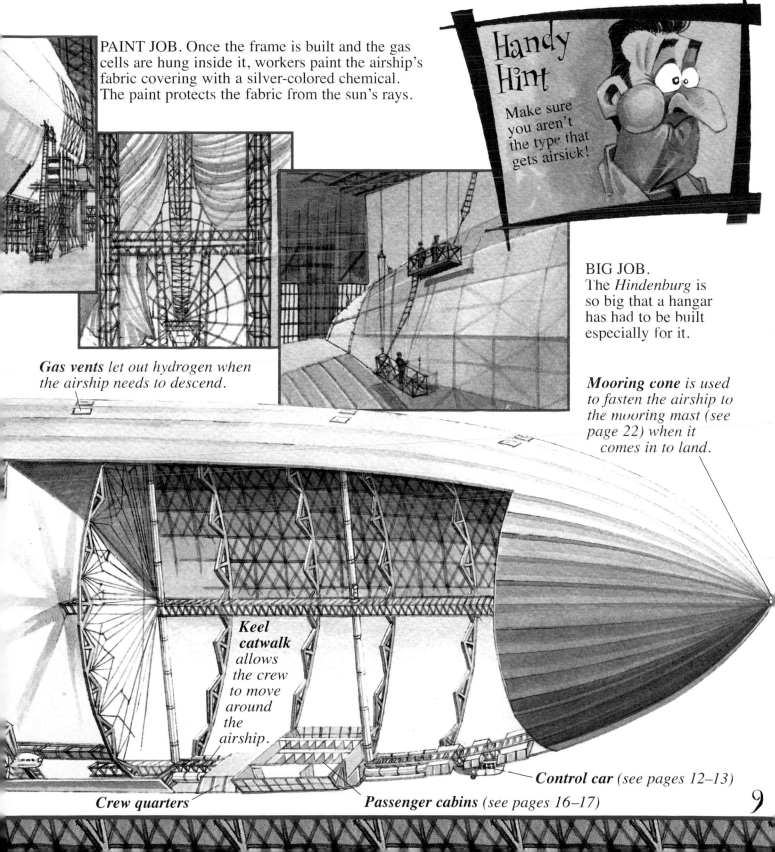

PAINT JOB. Once the frame is built and the gas cells are hung inside it, workers paint the airship's fabric covering with a silver-colored chemical. The paint protects the fabric from the sun's rays.

Handy Hint

Make sure you aren't the type that gets airsick!

BIG JOB. The *Hindenburg* is so big that a hangar has had to be built especially for it.

Gas vents let out hydrogen when the airship needs to descend.

Mooring cone is used to fasten the airship to the mooring mast (see page 22) when it comes in to land.

Keel catwalk allows the crew to move around the airship.

Crew quarters

Passenger cabins (see pages 16–17)

Control car (see pages 12–13)

All in a Day's Work

The *Hindenburg* carries a crew of 61. In addition to the captain and officers who command and fly the airship, there are teams of engineers, mechanics, and electricians. Cooks, stewards, and cabin boys keep the passengers happy.

When you are on duty, you work in one of the four engine cars. Your job is to keep the huge diesel engine running smoothly at the right speed. Officers in the control car send instructions to your engine telegraph, a big round instrument on the wall of the engine car. This tells you the speed to which you need to set the engine.

The Crew

FIVE CAPTAINS take turns commanding the airship.

THE WATCH OFFICER assists the captains.

NAVIGATORS keep the airship on course.

RADIO OFFICERS make contact with ground stations.

ENGINEERING OFFICERS look after the engines and systems.

THE ELEVATORMAN controls the elevator flaps that keep the airship level.

THE HELMSMAN steers the airship.

ELECTRICIANS look after the electrical systems.

ENGINE MECHANICS keep the engines running.

RIGGERS look after the airship's gas cells, bracing wires, and netting.

A STEWARDESS joins the crew in 1937.

SEVEN STEWARDS serve the passengers' meals and drinks.

A DOCTOR deals with minor injuries and illnesses.

FIVE COOKS prepare freshly cooked meals.

A CABIN BOY helps in the kitchen and does other small jobs.

Flying the Giant

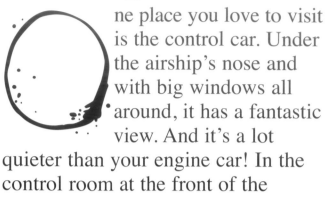

One place you love to visit is the control car. Under the airship's nose and with big windows all around, it has a fantastic view. And it's a lot quieter than your engine car! In the control room at the front of the control car, the helmsman steers the airship by turning a wheel that controls the rudders. The elevatorman turns another wheel to keep the ship level. Behind them in the navigation room, the navigator plots the airship's course. The radio officer works in the radio room, above the control car.

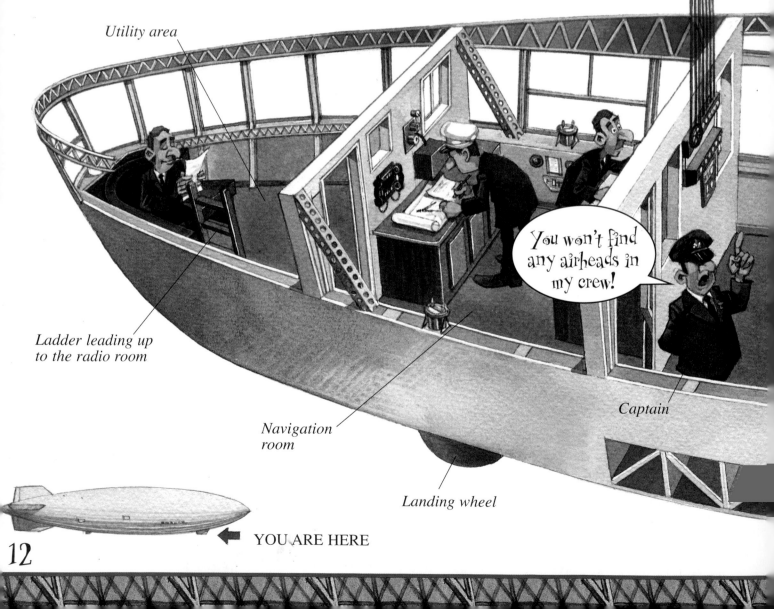

Utility area

Ladder leading up to the radio room

You won't find any airheads in my crew!

Captain

Navigation room

Landing wheel

YOU ARE HERE

THE RUDDERS (upper and lower) swivel to one side or the other to turn the airship.

THE ELEVATORS swivel up or down to raise or lower the airship's tail.

Elevator wheel

Lower rudder

Handy Hint

Don't light a match. Leaking hydrogen is extremely flammable—it might catch fire!

THE RADIO OFFICER reports the airship's position and receives weather reports.

Elevatorman

Helmsman

Control room

Rudder wheel

Pride of the Reich

Since 1933, Adolf Hitler has been in power in Germany. He and his Nazi government—known as the Third Reich—have provided money for the *Hindenburg* project.

One of the first flights you make in 1936 is over the opening ceremony of the Olympic Games in Berlin (shown at right). Hitler is now dictator (absolute ruler) of Germany, and he's eager to show off the power of the Third Reich. You're uneasy—and rightly so. Hitler will go on to start World War II and cause the death of millions.

IN RETURN for the Nazis' funding, the *Hindenburg* has to make propaganda flights for their government. You wish you didn't have to do this—you're sickened by Hitler's plans to rid Germany of anyone he considers inferior.

THE SWASTIKA, *the cross-shaped emblem of the Nazi party, is displayed on the* Hindenburg's *tail.*

Handy Hint

Learn to like thunderstorms. You're going to get very close to them!

It's raining paper!

At least it's not cats and dogs.

ON ITS FIRST passenger flight to Brazil, the *Hindenburg*'s passengers get a great view of Rio de Janeiro's giant statue of Jesus Christ, completed in 1931.

IN MARCH 1936, just before it leaves for Brazil, the *Hindenburg* has to fly across Germany, dropping leaflets and blaring out speeches in support of the Nazi government.

15

Inside the Hindenburg

Promenade

You like walking through the empty airship before the passengers arrive. Everything sparkles and gleams. You have to be careful not to let your oily overalls touch the polished furniture and crisp white tablecloths.

I wish my engine car looked like this...

THE DINING ROOM.
Passengers sit at tables set with fine china, expensive silverware, and freshly cut flowers.

Gangway

The passengers enter the *Hindenburg* by climbing up one of two gangways. Once everyone is onboard, the gangways fold up into the bottom of the airship.

First the passengers come to the lower deck, B-Deck. This is where the kitchen, toilets, and shower rooms are. The messrooms where the crew eat their meals are also on this deck. Another flight of stairs takes the passengers up to the bigger A-Deck. This houses the passenger cabins, dining room, and lounge.

16

Dining room

THE PASSENGER CABINS are comfortable but small. Each has two beds, one above the other.

Passenger cabin

Handy Hint

BRRR!

Wear warm clothes—it can be freezing cold in the engine cars.

Cutaway view of A-Deck

Lounge

This is the good life!

A SPACIOUS PROMENADE, or walkway, runs along each side of A-Deck, which is lined with big slanting windows.

THE LOUNGE has a huge map of the world on one wall, showing the voyages of great explorers in history.

17

Flying First Class

You couldn't afford to fly on the *Hindenburg* as a passenger. The fare is 400 U.S. dollars for a one-way ticket—about the same price as a car at this time! But then the *Hindenburg* is the most spacious and luxurious aircraft ever built. It's the best way to see the world's cities, floating just 650 to 1,000 feet (200 to 300 m) above the rooftops.

The passengers eat well, too. A chef tells you that the kitchen goes through about 440 pounds (200 kg) of fresh meat and poultry, 220 pounds (100 kg) of butter, and 800 eggs on a typical Atlantic flight taking less than three days.

I only fly first class.

THREE DELICIOUS MEALS a day are served by stewards in the airship's dining room.

THE KITCHEN spreads wonderful cooking smells throughout the airship as the chef prepares the passengers' meals.

Clickety clickety

THE READING AND WRITING ROOM has a typewriter for passengers to write letters.

PASSENGERS enjoy breathtaking views from the promenade windows.

THE LOUNGE PIANO is specially made of aluminum and pigskin to save weight.

EMILIE IMHOFF becomes the first zeppelin stewardess when she joins the *Hindenburg*'s crew for the 1937 season.

The Last Flight

It's May 3, 1937, and you are eager to get to work because the *Hindenburg* is leaving for its first flight of the year to the United States. So far it has flown more than 200,000 miles (320,000 km). This will be its 37th transatlantic flight. When you arrive at the new Rhein-Main World Airport near Frankfurt, Germany, the *Hindenburg*'s hangar is buzzing with visitors eager to see the giant airship. Only 36 passengers are making this trip, but the return flight to Europe will be full of people traveling to the coronation of King George VI in London.

THE LAST SUPPLIES are loaded early in the morning and final checks are made for the airship's departure in the evening.

MAY 3, LATE AFTERNOON: The *Hindenburg* is walked out of its hangar by the ground crew. Then the passengers begin boarding.

8:15 p.m.: You head out along the English Channel and across the Atlantic.

MAY 6, EARLY MORNING: Passengers spot the coast of Newfoundland. They can see icebergs floating in the dark sea.

Squeal!!

Squawk!

MAY 6, LATE MORNING: When the *Hindenburg* appears in the sky over American farms, some of the animals take fright and run about in panic.

3:00 p.m.: Photographers at the top of New York's Empire State Building take pictures of the *Hindenburg* as it flies past.

21

Lakehurst

When you reach the landing ground at Lakehurst, New Jersey, there is a delay of several hours to let a storm pass. At last you hear the order for the crew to prepare for landing. You can relax for now—you're off duty—but you're due to start work after the landing, preparing the engines for takeoff. The captain hopes this can be done quickly to make up for the delay.

Suddenly you hear a strange noise—a kind of muffled thud. Maybe it's the sound of a mooring line snapping? Or is it something more serious?

7:05 p.m.
The Hindenburg *turns at full speed.*

Mooring mast

THE *HINDENBURG* hangs motionless in the air. The ground crew gather to pick up the mooring lines so they can pull the giant airship to its mooring mast.

> I don't like the sound of that...

THUD!

THE FIRST SIGN of trouble noticed by people inside the airship is a bang and a sudden jolt. Everyone is puzzled by it.

Fire!

You run from the crew messroom on B-Deck into the airship's hull and look up. You can see a bright glow through gas cell number 4, near the tail. You realize right away that it's your worst nightmare: fire. It spreads quickly. Outside, people see a bright ball of flame bursting from the *Hindenburg*'s tail. The ground crew run for their lives. Within seconds, the whole airship is burning. As the hydrogen burns, the mighty airship sinks to the ground and its metal frame collapses. The whole disaster lasts only 32 seconds.

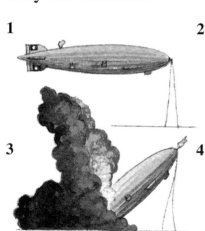

1

2

3

4

FLAMES are seen just in front of the tail. The tail end of the airship burns and sinks to the ground first, while the front stays afloat.

THE FIRE ROARS though the airship and bursts out of its nose. Finally, the gas cells at the front catch fire. The nose then falls to the ground.

Hindenburg

Handy Hint

Get to know the escape route you'd use in an emergency.

THE FIRE SPREADS so fast, you have to run to stay ahead of it.

Oh, the humanity!*

Run!

RADIO REPORTER Herbert Morrison is recording his description of the landing when he suddenly finds himself reporting the most important story of his career.

* actual words from Morrison's report

25

Escape

Inside the *Hindenburg*, the lounge tips up at a crazy angle. Tables and chairs go flying across the floor. Passengers reach for something to hold on to. You climb down as low as you can go inside the hull, staying underneath the raging inferno. When the hull hits the ground, a broken girder rips through the fabric, and you are thrown out to safety. Many other people also have lucky escapes. Amazingly, 62 of the 97 people onboard survive the disaster.

SOME PASSENGERS desperately jump from windows to get away from the fire. Sadly, many of them die because the airship is still too high above the ground. Most of those who wait until the airship is closer to the ground survive.

RICHARD KOLLMER, an engine mechanic like you, escapes by ripping open the fabric covering of the tail fin and stepping out through the hole.

IN THE LOUNGE, Margaret Mather pulls her coat around her face. She hears people calling to her from outside. She runs toward the sound of their voices and survives.

I can't see a thing!

Handy Hint

Don't panic! Keep calm and try to help others if you can.

My hero!

14-YEAR-OLD cabin boy Werner Franz jumps through a hatch to the ground, but he finds himself trapped amid fire and smoke. Then a water tank bursts above him. The water soaks him and also clears some of the smoke so he can see his way to safety.

27

What Went Wrong?

Everyone is talking about what might have caused the disaster. Some people think the fire may have been started deliberately by a bomb. Like some of the engineers and mechanics, you think a tight turn at full speed may have broken something inside the airship and torn open one of the gas cells. Gas pouring out could have been set on fire by the tiniest spark.

The official inquiry decides that gas leaking from a vent on top of the airship caught fire. Static electricity in the storm clouds—the same kind of electricity that makes lightning—may have caused sparks.

Leaking gas

All I know is I'm lucky to be alive!

FBI AGENTS question some of the crew and passengers, but they cannot find any evidence of crime or terrorism onboard the *Hindenburg*.

A PUBLIC INQUIRY begins in a hangar at the Lakehurst Naval Air Station only four days after the disaster.

Crackle!

Handy Hint

Tell the investigators everything you know, so that disasters can be avoided in the future.

Mooring mast

Crack!

WAS THE *HINDENBURG* destroyed by a bomb? A bomber might have used a timer, planning to be off the airship by the time the bomb exploded—but the late landing would have trapped the bomber onboard. However, the investigators find no trace of a bomb.

DID A BRACING WIRE SNAP and tear open a gas cell? We may never know for sure what brought the *Hindenburg* down.

Glossary

Altitude The height of something above sea level.

Anti-aircraft guns Guns built specially for shooting at aircraft.

Artillerymen Soldiers who fire big guns, called artillery.

Bracing wires Strong wires that held a zeppelin's frame in shape.

Catwalk A narrow, raised walkway.

Elevator Part of the tail that tilts up or down to make an airship climb higher, go lower, or stay level.

Elevatorman A crewman who controls the elevator flaps.

FBI The Federal Bureau of Investigation, the U.S. government's law-enforcement agency.

Field guns Artillery guns mounted on wheels so they can be moved around.

Gas cell A gas-filled bag inside an airship.

Gas vents Valves that can be opened like faucets to let gas out of the cells.

Girder A strong metal beam.

Hangar A large shelter or building with enough space inside to park one or more aircraft.

Hatch A doorway in a ship, submarine, or aircraft.

Helmsman A crewman who operates the helm, a wheel that controls the rudders.

Hull The body of a ship or airship.

Hydrogen The highly flammable, lighter-than-air gas that filled the *Hindenburg*'s gas cells and lifted the ship into the air.

Keel The strong beam that runs along the bottom of a ship or airship.

LZ Short for *Luftschiff Zeppelin*, German for "Zeppelin airship." Every Zeppelin airship had an LZ number. *Hindenburg*'s was LZ129.

Messroom A room where staff or crew eat their meals.

Mooring cone The tip of the airship's nose. When the airship lands, a steel cable from the mooring cone pulls the airship up to a mooring mast attached to the ground.

Mooring line A rope or cable let down from an airship when it is about to land. The lines are held by people on the ground, or tied to a mooring mast.

Mooring mast A short tower to which an airship is tied when it lands, to hold it steady on the ground.

Navigation Planning and directing the course of a vehicle.

Nazi party The political party that governed Germany from 1933 to 1945.

Propaganda Information that is given out to persuade people to support one point of view or one group of people.

Quarters Rooms or buildings where staff or passengers live.

Reich German for "empire." Nazi Germany, 1933–1945, was known as the Third Reich.

Rudder Part of the tail that swivels to one side or the other to steer an airship.

Steward A crew member who looks after passengers and serves their food and drinks.

Vent An opening for releasing gas from an airship. Airships like the *Hindenburg* vented (released) gas in order to reduce height before landing.

Zeppelin A type of airship named after its inventor, Count Ferdinand von Zeppelin.

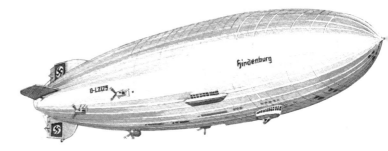

Index